MW01119779

Junk
Sculpture

Nicolas Brasch

NELSON
CENGAGE Learning

Australia • Brazil • Japan • Korea • Mexico • Singapore • Spain • United Kingdom • United States

Junk Sculpture

Text: Nicolas Brasch
Editor: Johanna Rohan
Design: Georgie Wilson
Reprint: Siew Han Ong

Acknowledgements
The author and publisher would like to acknowledge
permission to reproduce material from the following
sources:
Photographs by Australian Library/ Corbis/ AFP, p. 18
bottom/ Tony Arruza, p. 10 bottom/ Dave Bartruff, p. 7/
Nick Hawkes; Ecoscene, p. 6 centre/ Sally A. Morgan;
Econscene, p. 6 top/ Kevin Fleming, pp. 16, 16 bottom/ Mark
E. Gibson, p. 12 top/ Dave G. Houser, p.18 top/ Ronnie
Kaufman, p. 19 top/ Layne Kennedy, p. 12 Bottom/ Maren
Hunt Mason, p. 29 bottom right/ Ricki Rosen, p. 6 bottom;
Lindsay Edwards, back cover, pp.9, 11, 13, ,14, 15, 17, 19, 22-23;
Getty Images/ Imagebank, front cover top, 4 top/ Stone,
front cover bottom, p.4 bottom; 20 bottom left;
Photolibrary.com, 20 top.

**PM Extras Non-Fiction
Emerald**
How Does Your Garden Grow?
Working with Wood
How Magic Tricks Work
Junk Sculpture
Spin, Weave, Knit and Knot
The Puppet Show

Text © 2004 Cengage Learning Australia Pty Limited
Illustrations © 2004 Cengage Learning Australia Pty Limited

Copyright Notice
This Work is copyright. No part of this Work may be reproduced, stored in a
retrieval system, or transmitted in any form or by any means without prior
written permission of the Publisher. Except as permitted under the
Copyright Act 1968, for example any fair dealing for the purposes of private
study, research, criticism or review, subject to certain limitations. These
limitations include: Restricting the copying to a maximum of one chapter or
10% of this book, whichever is greater; Providing an appropriate notice and
warning with the copies of the Work disseminated; Taking all reasonable
steps to limit access to these copies to people authorised to receive these
copies; Ensuring you hold the appropriate Licences issued by the Copyright
Agency Limited ("CAL"), supply a remuneration notice to CAL and pay any
required fees.

For product information and technology assistance,
**in Australia call 1300 790 853;
in New Zealand call 0508 635 766**

For permission to use material from this text or product,
please email **aust.permissions@cengage.com**

ISBN 978 0 17 011436 3
ISBN 978 0 17 011434 9 (set)

Cengage Learning Australia
Level 7, 80 Dorcas Street
South Melbourne, Victoria Australia 3205

Cengage Learning New Zealand
Unit 4B Rosedale Office Park
331 Rosedale Road, Albany, North Shore NZ 0632

For learning solutions, visit **cengage.com.au**

Printed in China by 1010 Printing International Ltd
12 15

Contents

Recycled Materials

One person's junk is another person's treasure. Making sculptures with recycled materials saves money and is a lot of fun. Recycled materials are used for one purpose and then used again for something else. There is almost no limit to the different materials that can be re-used when creating a sculpture. If you find an object you don't think you can use, close your eyes and let your imagination run wild!

What is a Sculpture?

A sculpture is a **three-dimensional** object created to be looked at and admired. Some sculptures can also be climbed upon, touched or used to store things in.

A Recycled Joke

It is not only objects that are recycled. Jokes can be recycled too.

Q - Why did the chicken cross the road?

A - To get to the other side.

Maybe jokes like this shouldn't be recycled, though!

People who use recycled materials to make sculptures are helping the environment. When materials are thrown away, they are either buried or burnt. When materials are buried, they take up a lot of land that could be used for other purposes. When materials are burnt, they create gases that harm the environment. When making sculptures, it is important to remember to **reduce, reuse** and **recycle**.

Collecting Recycled Materials

Keep your eyes open to spot materials that you can use. You may hear other people talking about materials that they have seen but not picked up. Don't think that using recycled materials is second best. Many **professional sculptors** only use recycled materials.

Here are some materials that can be recycled and used in sculpting.

- Newspapers
- Bottles
- Fabric
- Cotton reels
- Egg cartons
- Cards
- Wire
- Computer parts
- CDs
- Wood

Recycling Tip

Before you start sculpting, put on an old shirt. This is really getting into the spirit of recycling!

Before you start collecting old materials to make sculptures from, it is a good idea to set up a storage system. Collect some large boxes and put labels on them. Each box should be for one particular material. Before storing the materials that you have collected, make sure that you wash them well.

A Piñata

A piñata is a **papier-mâché** figure that is usually full of sweets. It comes from Mexico, where it is used at festivals and celebrations. People are blindfolded and given a stick. They take turns to hit the piñata, which is hung from a rope. The piñata is full of sweets. When it splits open all the children rush forward and grab the sweets.

Here are the materials that are needed to make a piñata:

- **paper (magazines, newspapers, wrapping paper)**
- **a balloon • glue • paint • paintbrushes • scissors • sweets**

How do you turn the materials into a piñata?

1. Blow up the balloon and tie a knot in it.
2. Tear some of the paper into strips and soak them in a container of craft glue and water.
3. Paste them onto the balloon until the balloon is covered.
4. Let the paper dry overnight, then glue more strips of paper on.
5. Paint the piñata in bright colours.
6. When the paint is dry, cut a hole in the top with some scissors, and fill it up with sweets.

A Cardboard City

Almost everyone has cardboard lying around the house. It may be from old cereal boxes, greeting cards or packaging inside a parcel. Some of this cardboard may have already been recycled several times. Old cardboard is often sent to a recycling **plant**.

At the plant, the old cardboard is **pulped** and turned into a liquid. It is then spread out and dried. When it is dry, it is cut into new sheets of cardboard.

Here are the materials that are needed to make a cardboard city:

• **sheets of cardboard** • **scissors** • **glue** • **paint** • **paintbrushes**

How do you turn the materials into a cardboard city?

1. Place a large sheet of cardboard on a table.
2. Cut the sheets up into rectangles of different sizes. These are the buildings.
3. Glue the buildings onto the large sheet of cardboard. Start with the big rectangles, then glue the smaller ones on top.
4. Paint windows, doors and signs onto the buildings.

An Egg Carton Monster

Egg cartons are a fantastic shape. The bumps and holes make them great fun to use in a sculpture. Have you ever had a close look at the bottom half of an egg carton? If you put two of them together they could be the jaws and teeth of a monster or a crocodile. Snap! Snap!

A Piece of Advice

When cutting up egg cartons, there is one important thing to remember. Make sure that there are no eggs left inside. Otherwise you are going to end up with a huge mess!

Here are the materials that are needed to make an egg carton monster:

- **three egg cartons** • **a small cardboard box** • **scissors** • **tape**
- **glue** • **paint** • **paintbrushes** • **a small rope**

How do you turn the materials into an egg carton monster?

1. Remove the top of the egg cartons.
2. Tape the two cartons together at one end, so that they form an open jaw.
3. Glue the jaw to one end of the cardboard box.
4. Cut four of the egg holders from the other carton and glue them to the bottom of the box to make the feet.
5. Tape the rope to the other end of the box to make the tail.
6. Paint the monster in bright, ferocious colours.

A Chinese Dragon

In China, the dragon is considered a symbol of good luck. At Chinese New Year celebrations, dancers climb under a large dragon costume. They perform the Chinese Dragon Dance. At the end of the dance, they let off firecrackers. The dragon costume is made up of a head, long body and tail. By tying together soft drink cans, you can create your own Chinese dragon. If you pull it along the ground, it will make a lot of noise.

Here are the materials that are needed to make a Chinese dragon:

- **used soft drink cans** • **a hammer and nail** • **glue**
- **a very long piece of string** • **cardboard** • **paint** • **paintbrushes**

How do you turn the materials into a Chinese dragon?

1. Carefully nail a hole in the bottom of each can.
2. Thread the cans onto the piece of string.
3. When the last can is on, tie a knot at the end.
4. Paint some eyes and a long fiery, tongue on the cardboard. Cut them out and glue them onto the first can.
5. Paint some scales on the cardboard, cut them out and glue them onto the second and third cans.

A Fabric Hat

Some hats are worn to protect people from the sun, and some hats are worn to keep the rain off. However, some hats are worn simply for decoration. On special occasions, people wear hats because they want to be noticed and admired. People wear hats at weddings, parties and the Melbourne Cup! These kinds of hats are really works of art. A recycled fabric hat is also a work of art. It can be worn, but it can also be hung up and admired.

Here are the materials that are needed to make a fabric hat:

- tape measure • cardboard • tape • glue
- fabric (all shapes, sizes and colours)

How do you turn the materials into a fabric hat?

1. Measure the distance around the top of your head.
2. Cut out a strip of cardboard the same length as your head measurement and 10 centimetres wide.
3. Glue one end of the cardboard to the other, to form a circle. This is the base of the hat.
4. Cut out a large, square piece of cardboard and glue one side of the base to it.
5. Glue the fabric onto the square cardboard until it is a mass of fabric.

Wire Figures

Wire is very **flexible**. It can be twisted into many different shapes and it can be easily cut to any size. Wire can be used to hang things from, or can hang from other objects. Some wire is easier to work with than other wire. Coat hangers are made from wire but they are hard to twist and bend. Wire that is used to hang up pictures may be too thin and floppy to use. The wire in pipe cleaners is flexible and easy to bend. Whenever you see some spare wire, pick it up, bend it and twist it. Often, experimenting with materials is the best way to learn which ones to use.

Safety Tip

Always bend the end of the wire into a small loop so it doesn't poke anyone.

Here are the materials that are needed to make a wire figure:

- **pipe cleaners** - **scissors or wire cutters**

How do you turn the materials into wire figures?

1. Bend the pipe cleaners to form the different parts of the body.
2. Form a head by making a small loop.
3. Form the legs by bending a pipe cleaner in the middle.
4. Form the arms by cutting a pipe cleaner into two small, straight pieces and attaching them to the piece that forms the body.

A Little Bit of Everything

So far, you have seen how many different types of materials can be recycled and used in sculptures. When you want to make a sculpture, have a look around your house and garden. You may find lots of objects and materials to use. For example, old CDs can be tied together to form a mobile. Pinecones can be decorated with paint and glitter. Paper bags can be blown up and painted. Let your imagination run wild!

WIRE

CDs

FABRIC

NEWSPAPERS

Glossary

flexible	easily bent or changed
papier-mâché	a work of art made from pieces of paper glued together in layers
plant	a factory
professional	someone who is paid for doing particular jobs
pulped	moistened and crushed
recycle	to use something again
reduce	to make smaller in number
reuse	to use something more than once
sculptors	people who create sculptures
three-dimensional	something with height, width and depth

Further Reading

Ansell, Hilary, *Art of Recycling*, Folens Belair Publications, London, 2000.

Fiarotta, Phyllis and Noel, *Cups and Cans and Paper Plate Fans*, Sterling Publishing, USA, 1992.

Kohl, MaryAnn and Gainer, Cindy, *Good Earth Art*, Bright Ring Publishing, USA, 1991.